Exploring da Vinci's Last Supper

Catherine McGrew Jaime

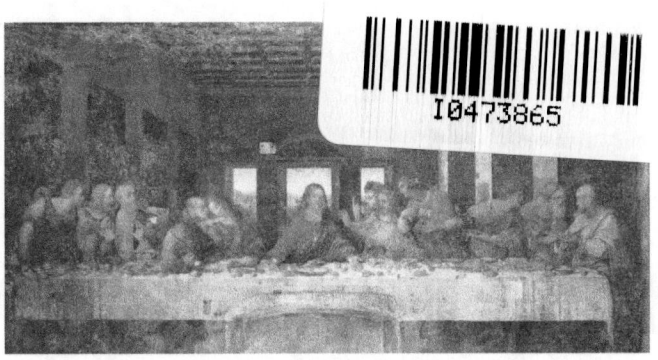

Leonardo da Vinci, 1498

Other Books by Catherine Jaime

Da Vinci: His Life and His Legacy
Doing Da Vinci for Kids
Leonardo the Florentine (historical fiction)
Leonardo: Masterpieces in Milan (historical fiction)
Leonardo: To Mantua and Beyond
A Brief History of New York City
A Brief Financial History of the United States
Understanding the Electoral College
A Brief Introduction to the Lewis and Clark Expedition
York Proceeded On (historical fiction)
Tales from the Troubled South: Civil Rights in Alabama
An American Looks at Wuerzburg, Germany
A Trial of a Trial (A Mock Trial Story)
A Novel Approach to Shakespeare's Much Ado About Nothing

Creative Learning Connection

8006 Old Madison Pike, Ste 11-A
Madison, Alabama 35758
U.S.A.

www.CreativeLearningConnection.com

Table of Contents

Introduction

When most of us hear the term "The Last Supper" we think immediately of Leonardo da Vinci's painting. In fact, it would appear on most people's "most famous paintings in the world" lists – often just above or below the *Mona Lisa*.

And yet, da Vinci was neither the first **nor** the most recent to make a painting of this particular subject. And after over five hundred years of deterioration, his is certainly not in the best condition. Additionally, it has never been moved (though at least one French king proposed the idea); and it has never been stolen, an act that was instrumental in causing a rise in popularity to da Vinci's *Mona Lisa* (but that's a story for another day).

And yet, there it is, an icon of a religious event that is well known among many who are religious **and** many who are not!

"One of You Shall Betray Me."

In the New Testament, the four gospels of Matthew, Mark, Luke and John all mention the moment that Leonardo portrays in his painting of the *Last Supper*, the moment during the Passover meal when Christ alarms his disciples by announcing, "Verily I say unto you, that one of you shall betray me."

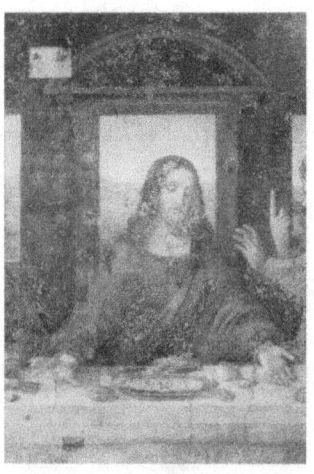

Here's how Leonardo chose to portray the event: He put Christ in the center, with a window behind him, giving him the effect of a halo, without actually including one. Christ is the focal point of the picture, with his head and hands making a triangle (often seen as the symbol of perfection, and of the trinity).

Christ's robe is blue and red, which can be seen to indicate his divine side and his earthly side. Even the appearance of his hands coincides with that – the one on the "earthly" side is clenched, as if anticipating his death on the cross, and the one on his left (our right) is open wide, possibly indicating his openness to the sacrifice he is about to give. Christ's mouth is partially open as if he just uttered the words.

Due to the door cut out in the bottom of the *Last Supper*, we can no longer for sure tell how Leonardo painted Christ's feet, but preparatory drawings (and copies made soon after its completion) show his feet crossed, as they would later be on the cross.

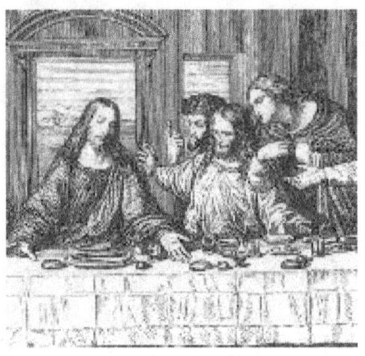

Da Vinci then groups the disciples in groups of three, with each group reacting to the surprise announcement. On Christ's immediate left, James the Elder is drawing back in terror, Thomas is advancing towards Christ with a raised finger, and

Philip rises, bending forward, laying his hand on his own chest. Thomas can be seen as asking "Who is the traitor" or "Are you sure?" His raised finger could also represent after Christ has risen, and Doubting Thomas says he won't believe until he has put his finger in the nail wounds.

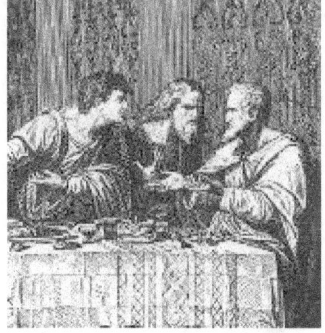

The second group on Christ's left are conversing with each other. Matthew unites the group, extending his hands towards the Savior. Thaddeus shows surprise, doubt, and suspicion. Simon is deep in thought and appears troubled.

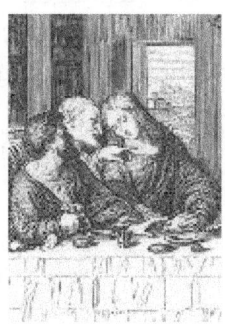

To the immediate right of Christ are John, the youngest of the disciples (who bends towards

Peter, the eldest of the disciples), Judas (holding the purse with the money he has received for betraying Christ), and Peter grasping the right shoulder of John. Peter is holding a knife that "accidently" touches Judas, as Judas overturns a salt-cellar at the surprising announcement. It looks like Peter is asking John a question that John doesn't know the answer to.

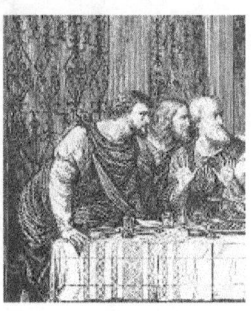

At the other end of the table Bartholomew is standing, bending forward with both his hands on the table, as if he is trying to understand. James the Younger (the most damaged portion of the painting) has his hand on Peter's shoulder, and Andrew appears horrified at the thought of betrayal, and as if he wants to declare himself innocent. His eyes show astonishment and fear.

Pictorial Representations
of the *Last Supper*
by Several Other Artists

Earlier than Leonardo da Vinci's

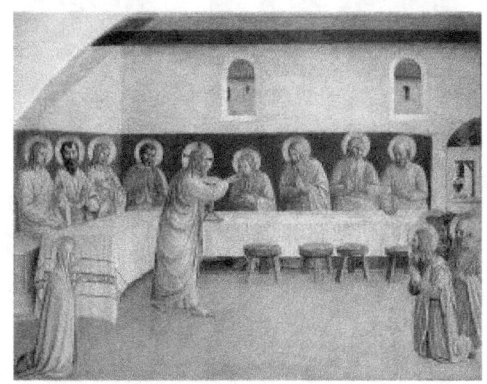

Fra Angelico, 1440

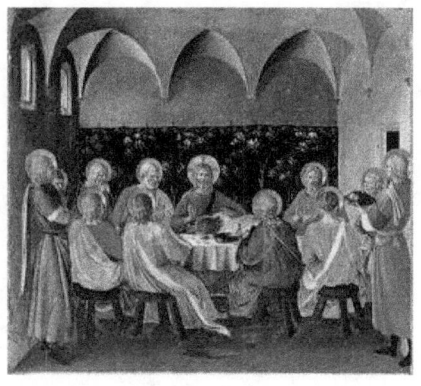

Armadio degli Argenti, 1451 – 1453 (39 x 37 cm)

Contempary with Da Vinci's

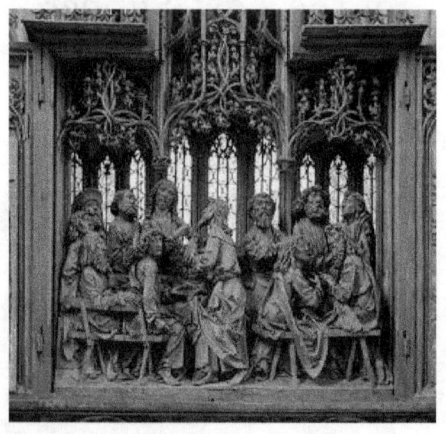

Tilman Riemenschneider, 1501-1502

Later Than Da Vinci's

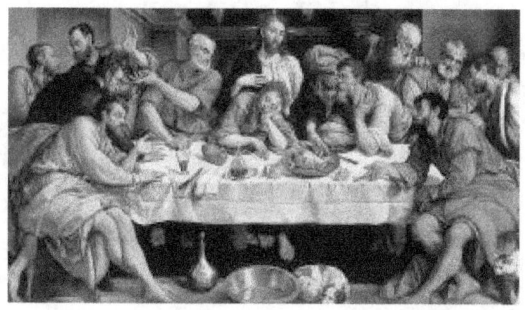

Jacopo Bassano, 1542

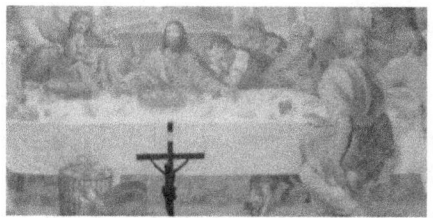

Ottavio Semino, ~ 1560

And these are just a handful of literally dozens (if not hundreds) of representations of the *Last Supper*, before and after da Vinci painted his.

The History of the Da Vinci's Last Supper

The following is from the Last Supper chapter of the non-fiction work, Da Vinci: His Life and His Legacy.

In 1495, three years after Columbus discovered the New World, Leonardo da Vinci started his *Last Supper* mural for the monks' dining room at the Santa Maria delle Grazie. (Donato Bramante was working on the dome there at the same time.) The Last Supper was a popular theme for frescos before and since his day, but Leonardo chose to do it in a unique manner – painting the disciples in groups of three at the table, each reacting to Christ's statement, "One of you will betray me." Additionally, he chose to depict "modern day" clothes, foods, and dishes for the picture, instead of those from the New Testament era, so that the monks there could relate better to it.

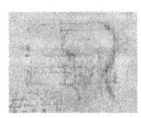

Quote by Leonardo da Vinci in one of his journals: "When you wish to represent a man speaking to a number of people, consider the matter of which he has to treat and adapt his action to the subject. Thus if he speaks persuasively, let his action be appropriate to it..."

Even before he could start painting, Leonardo had to do countless sketches in preparation. He wanted each detail to be perfect. He agonized the longest over the faces for Christ and for Judas. One story is that he had to go to the worst part of Milan to find a face horrible enough to use for his model of Judas.

Another legend is that he inadvertently used the same person as his model for both Christ and Judas, a man who had become hardened in the years between the two portions of the picture. Christ and Judas were the last two faces he did so not much time separated the painting of the two of them, and so that story is unlikely. And yet a third legend is that the head monk complained to Leonardo that he was taking too long to finish the painting, and Leonardo offered to use HIS face for the model for Judas...bringing an end to that complaint.

Unfortunately, the *Last Supper* was yet another of Leonardo's experiments, since he didn't like the current way of painting frescos. Fresco painting techniques required an artist to apply wet plaster to a section of a wall, and then paint that section quickly with water-based paints. This method effectively bonded the paint to the plaster – which is why even after centuries, frescoes done this way have vibrant colors.

Leonardo wanted to paint slowly, and to be able to make changes as he went along. He developed a new paint solution of varnish and oil which he could use on a dry wall and change along the way. Because Leonardo was a perfectionist, and was distracted by other projects, he spent many years working on the mural. Sadly, Leonardo had not perfected his new technique, and even in his lifetime the paint of his incredible *Last Supper* mural began to flake off the wall.

In 1652, monks cut a door in the wall where the *Last Supper* is painted, cutting out the feet of Christ in the process. At another point, in 1796, French soldiers under Napoleon staying in the monastery defaced the painting by throwing things at it.

During World War II, the wall was reinforced, and sand bags were placed behind the wall with the painting. A bomb hit the monastery only a few feet away from the wall, fortunately causing no more damage to the painting.

The Last Supper is a masterpiece, and ranks with Leonardo's *Mona Lisa* for the fame associated with it. Even in Leonardo's lifetime, it was appreciated. When the French King, Louis XII, saw the painting, he was so impressed by it – he wanted to take it back to France – wall and all! Obviously not a practical idea, so the painting stayed where it was. All over the world, copies of it hang on home and church walls alike.

Painting the *Last Supper*

*This section is a fictionalized (but very historically accurate)
account of the painting of the* Last Supper.
It is excerpted from Leonardo: Masterpieces in Milan.

Soon after the Duke and Duchess returned from
Vigevano, the Duke surprised Leonardo by asking
him to paint a mural in the Santa Maria delle
Grazie Church. Leonardo was surprised that with
all the other tasks the Duke had assigned him, that
he would add one more important job to those he
was already doing. But the Duke was now paying
his salary full-time, as well as that of several of his
apprentices, and if that's what the Duke desired,
Leonardo would surely do his best to comply.

Leonardo walked over to the church to see the
space he would be painting. A large wall, thirty feet
across and fourteen feet high, in the Dining Room
lay bare, awaiting the touch of the master.
Leonardo walked around the room, taking in the
wall from numerous angles. "Yes, I will paint the
Last Supper on that wall. It will be an appropriate
picture for the monks to view as they sup here."

As Leonardo contemplated the task, he took out
his omnipresent notebook and began to sketch
some ideas of how to display Christ and the
disciples in the painting. The first few pictures
were not to his liking, but then he struck on an idea
that did appeal to him. He would capture the
moment at which Christ had told the disciples that

one of them would betray him. With that decision, the sketches came quicker as he drew out the disciples, huddled in groups of three, as they contemplated the horror of such a thing.

Leonardo quickly decided he would dress the disciples in contemporary clothing, so that the monks could more easily identify with them, rather than in the costumes of Christ's day, as was the tradition with most painters.

Once again, the pressure started almost immediately for Leonardo to begin and then complete the painting quickly. But, for this project, Leonardo would not be rushed, not even for the Duke.

Leonardo abhorred the usual wet plaster method of painting frescoes, since it required working quickly. Most fresco painters combined their paint with plaster, and applied it to the surface quickly, so that the work could be done before the plaster dried.

But Leonardo would not paint anything quickly and therefore refused to use that method. He wanted to be able to paint his mural slowly, to make adjustments as he went along. He had been experimenting with a new method of painting murals that used a mixture of varnish and oil that would allow him to paint that way, and that's the method he planned to employ here.

As Leonardo finished his preliminary drawings of the disciples and the table in from of them, he slowly started to transfer the figures to the wall in the Dining Room. Even when only the cartoon (the drawings) had been done on the wall, people would stop to look in astonishment. Even without paint, it was as if the larger-than-life disciples were speaking and as if one could reach out and touch the Passover food on the table. All were anxious to see the work completed.

But Leonardo would not be rushed. He wanted the colors to be just right. He wanted to make sure the expressions on their faces were perfect. He would not be hurried by anyone, not even an impatient Duke or a set of frustrated monks. They would have to put up with the mess in the Dining Room longer. He had not asked for this assignment, but if he was going to do it, he was going to do it on his timetable, and he was going to do it well.

When Leonardo finally started painting, he began with the table and the table settings, finishing the food and the blue designs on the edges of the white tablecloth last.

He started work on the twelve disciples in the various groupings of three that he planned to display them in. He had pondered how best to show them, and had considered how little he knew about most of them. He had always found Peter to be a fellow of conflicted emotions with his insistence of perfect obedience to Jesus, and yet his denials of him within a week of this dinner. But he particularly liked the story of Peter's attempted defense of the Master in the garden when he cut off the ear of one of the arresting soldiers. And so, Leonardo had found himself drawing a small knife in Peter's hand. It could be seen as part of the meal, intended only for the cutting of the bread they were sharing, but for Leonardo it would hold a double meaning.

Of course, Leonardo knew that Judas would be an especially important part of the painting, and he put him in the same grouping with Peter, turned to look at Jesus. Leonardo wanted the face of Judas to show the anger and betrayal that he must have felt inside, even if no one else there had been aware of it. Leonardo carefully posed him, looking straight at Jesus. Judas would need no dagger in his hand; he had daggers in his eyes. Leonardo had searched the streets of Milan for many months, looking for just the right face to sketch for the model of this disciple.

With Peter and Judas carefully painted, Leonardo considered the color combinations he would use in each of the disciples' robes. He was always very meticulous about his color choices, knowing that the right choices would mean everything in the outcome of his mural. Several other artists had painted the *Last Supper* in subdued colors, as if they wanted the painting to fade into the background of the wall it covered, but not Leonardo. He wanted his colors to be bright and vivid. If he was going to be tasked with such a project as this, all who entered this dining room in the future should be drawn to the painting.

Leonardo mixed the various colored powders he planned to use on the mural that day. He only planned to paint a small section of one disciple at this point. Even with all the pressure from the monks and the Duke to complete this project sooner rather than later, Leonardo still would not be rushed. Each disciple would be painstakingly painted, as if he was the only person that counted in that group. Only then would Leonardo move on to the next disciple and then on to the next.

Leonardo planned to focus on their torsos first, and come back to the legs and feet that could be seen protruding from under the tablecloth later. He would not need as many colors for the lower portion of the painting, since there he would primarily be painting feet and sandals.

As Leonardo painstakingly applied the paint to the sandals of the disciples, Leonardo tried to remember the Bible stories he had heard somewhere along the way. Had Jesus washed the disciples' feet before or after they had partaken of this meal? He just couldn't remember. But regardless, he thought of that story as he painted the thirteen sets of feet. Feet shod only in sandals would have been dirty feet to wash indeed.

When Leonardo tired of work on the mural, he would wander outside to watch Donato Bramante's work on the dome…

Leonardo turned back to his art with a vengeance after his mother's death. His appearances at the church where he had been painting the Last Supper mural became more frequent. He could often be found on his scaffolding, tirelessly painting or repainting one small section, and then another.

As he stood in the middle of the room taking in the large painting, he could almost hear the conversations in the little groups of three as they discussed the shocking remarks that Jesus had just made. Now that the people were complete, and his focus had come back, he was ready to finish their surroundings. Leonardo first sketched out the walls surrounding the large table, the two side walls and the back wall in the distance.

Now he climbed up on his scaffolding to draw these backgrounds onto the wall itself. On each side wall he was placing four red-colored tapestries. He had considered making each tapestry unique, but he didn't want to take away from the central figures of the painting, and had decided instead on geometric patterns on each of them.

That would give them depth and interest without making them overwhelm the people. Between the tapestries would be doorways leading to the unknown.

Finally, he drew in the windows on the rear wall of the painting. Here he included a small portion of the landscape behind, again not wanting to detract from the people in the painting, but wanting to give the picture completeness.

When the walls had been completely drawn in, Leonardo turned his attention to the ceiling in the picture. He planned to give the ceiling a three-dimensional feel with a simple lattice-work design across the top of the room. Again, it would help complete the setting without competing with the focus.

With the background of the *Last Supper* complete, Leonardo made a few final finishing touches on the painting. He had completed the table portion much earlier, but now he wanted the orange slices and fish to be more vivid. Then Leonardo set down his brushes and stepped back from the project. After so many years of working on it, he was ready to call it finished. Even after all this time with students and apprentices, he normally did his own clean up, but for once he didn't feel like cleaning up after himself. Leonardo took off his work apron, and motioned to his apprentices who had been watching from nearby. They came forward quickly, and started the tedious cleaning process. Meanwhile, Leonardo walked to the far side of the dining room, to take one last look at his work, and walked out of the room...

More Details on the Painting Itself

Leonardo's mural is painted on a wall in the dining hall of the Santa Maria delle Grazie Monastery. The usual method to do murals was to fresco them, but Leonardo tried to paint the wall more like he painted on wood – so that he could make changes to it as he went.

The room is approximately 120 feet by 30 feet. The painting occupies most of the north wall (approximately 30 feet by 15 feet). The painting starts about eight to ten feet above the ground in the dining room. Windows on the left side of the room let in the late day light, lighting up all the faces except that of Judas (which stayed dark).

The figures are about fifty percent larger than life size (and Christ is slightly larger than the rest of the disciples). If standing completely, Leonardo's figures would be nine feet tall. Leonardo used proportion to do such a good job of enlarging the figures as much as he did. He also used perspective to accentuate Christ in the middle of the painting, as well as His size (He is slightly larger than the disciples), and the window behind him (rather than the traditional halo). The hands and faces show the disciples' emotions at Christ's shocking announcement.

The Painting over Time

The monastery was started in 1462, and enlarged in 1490. In 1495 Leonardo da Vinci was assigned to paint the mural at one end of the dining room, and another painter was assigned to fresco the other end at the same time. The fresco across from da Vinci's was done in the Tuscany style, hasn't been preserved at all, and yet today is more vibrant.

Even in Leonardo's lifetime, the painting was starting to deteriorate, and in 1556 Giorgio Vasari, the art historian, referred to the painting as merely a "muddle of blots."

The *Last Supper* has suffered greatly since then as well. The monks wanted to protect it at one point, and hung a curtain over it, opening it only for special visitors. Unfortunately, the curtain scratched the painting as it went back and forth. In addition, it trapped moisture between the curtain and the wall, causing more damage.

Over the centuries, starting in the 18th century, and then again in the 19th century, many artists have attempted to "restore" the *Last Supper*, often making the situation worse in the process. A major restoration was begun in 1977. An artist, Dr. Pinin Brambilla Barcilon, worked on the mural with a small microscope, removing centuries of dirt and grime, and the extra paint that had been applied since Leonardo's day. Twenty-two years later, she finally finished the project, which unfortunately met with mixed reviews from art critics around the world. Some thought she had gone too far with the removal of the paint, though others thought she had done an incredible job. (Having seen the painting recently, I go with the latter position – she did a remarkable job.)

By 1550 or so, a traveler wrote of the painting that it was "half spoiled"; another spoke of it as "lost" and another as "quite gone." In time, the cracks it increased, and quickly began to run together.

In 1652 a large door into the room was added, destroying the feet of Christ and several of the disciples. Additionally, the hammering and chiseling on the wall to make the door caused more damage to the painting.

Sometime around 1726, Pietro Bellotti, an inferior painter, offered to restore the painting, and proceeded to cover the entire thing with paint…and at other times it was partially touched up with watercolors. By 1770 Giuseppe Mazza had been hired to "fix" the painting. He scraped the painting and prepared to add paint himself, redoing all but three of the heads.

In 1796 Napoleon Bonaparte came through Milan with his army. After visiting the painting, he ordered that no damage be done to it and that the military stay out of the room. But he had no sooner left than another general arrived, breaking open the door and converting the dining room into a stable for the military's horses. (There was more mold damage to the painting as a result.)

Other problems were caused for the painting because the wall it is on is not far from the kitchen…and the convent is not built on a high place in Milan. In 1800 excessive rain caused water in the convent to be more than two feet high, causing serious problems for the painting.

In 1807 Prince Eugene (Beauharnais), the Viceroy of the Kingdom of Italy, ordered that the *Last Supper* should be repaired and repainted. Windows were added to the room, the dining hall was aired out and dried, and the floor removed. He had a layer of charcoal laid down to repel humidity.

Within the next few years, magistrates succeeded in shutting off the door and walling up the entrance to the dining room. For a time the only way to see the painting was to descend into the room by a ladder from the pulpit.

During World War II, the wall was reinforced, and sand bags were placed behind the wall with the painting. In 1943 Milan was bombed, and a bomb did hit the monastery only a few feet away from the right wall, fortunately causing no more damage to the painting nor to Bramante's dome. (The left side of the chapel was destroyed at that time.)

Today, there is only twenty percent of the original color left in the *Last Supper* painting.

Copies of da Vinci's *Last Supper*

Marco da Oggino one of da Vinci's students, made a small copy of da Vinci's mural about 1515 so that he could then make a larger copy on the wall of the convent of Castellazzo.

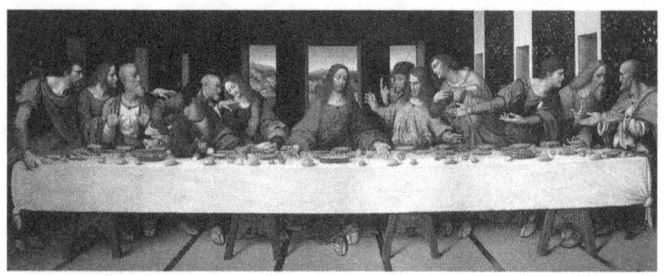

This copy is sometimes attributed to Oggiono, and sometimes to Giampietrino, another member of Leonardo's studio.

Sometime before 1565 another copy was made in fresco by Pietro Lovino at Ponte Capriasca. One of the changes he made was to put their names under each disciple. And in 1612 Andrea Bianchi (Vespino) was hired by Cardinal Frederick Borromeo to make a full size copy of it, so that it would not be lost forever.

In the late 1700's Raffaello Morghen made an engraving of the *Last Supper*, though it appears to have been based on Oggino's copy, rather than da Vinci's original.

In 1807 Giuseppe Bossi was ordered by the Viceroy to help make a mosaic copy of Leonardo's mural. He made a full size cartoon after looking at every copy of da Vinci's *Last Supper* he could find (apparently more than twenty). He mostly referenced the full size copy by Vespino. Once the cartoon was completed Bossi had a piece of canvas prepared and then sketched the entire painting on it. Then Bossi painted the sky/landscape, and then the head of Christ and three of the disciples. Bossi got ill before he could complete the sketch and went back to studying the information available from previous copies and authors of da Vinci's day. When he was done a mosaic was made based on his work, approximately 28 feet long and 18 feet high.

Final Thoughts

Leonardo worked on the *Last Supper* slowly as was his custom for any project, but it is also important to remember that this wasn't the only responsibility he had during those years He was also designing a larger than life equestrian monument for the Duke, while planning elaborate pageants, consulting on architectural issues, and much more. So the amazing thing may really be how much he managed to accomplish during his Milan years – including this massive painting, rather than how long it took him to finish this amazing mural.

I hope this small work has helped you to appreciate Leonardo da Vinci's *Last Supper* a bit more.

About the Author

Catherine has been researching and teaching about Leonardo da Vinci for over a decade. It started as a simple ten-week course on this interesting subject, and ten years later she is still going strong. The more she learns about da Vinci, the more she wants to learn, and the more she wants to share.

Catherine originally wrote a non-fiction book on Leonardo da Vinci, as well as several mini-units for students. But soon her interest led her to trying her hand at her first historical fiction on this exciting topic. As of October 2012, she had completed three novels on da Vinci, and had started research on a fourth.

The second novel included the time period when da Vinci painted the *Last Supper*. While doing research for that novel, Catherine had the opportunity to travel to see a da Vinci exhibit that focused primarily on the *Last Supper*. From that exhibit and her research for her novel, came this small booklet in 2011.

A surprise opportunity to travel to Italy with a couple of family members during the summer of 2012 and the chance to see the *Last Supper* in person led to several updates to this little booklet.